THIS IMAGINARY PLACE

ISBN #: 978-1-312-34385-6

Copyright © 2014 MJ Di Rocco
All Rights Reserved. No part of this publication may be reproduced, stored in a retrieval system, or transmitted, in any form or in any means – by electronic, mechanical, photocopying, recording or otherwise – without prior written permission.

Cover Photo By Tomo Miyagi Copyright © 2014 Used with permission

THIS IMAGINARY PLACE

M.J. Di Rocco

THE SILENT STORM

There is nothing here.
No feeling, no light.
Only the thunder of silent storm.
It rages,
The silent storm,
Where I hope to find you waiting for me.

I look to the sky,
For some distant sign of the storm.
I must be saved,
I must find the storm.

I have no words.
I can only run into the storm

The storm is carrying you on its back
Carrying you to me.
Carrying you to my salvation.

MY ILLUSION

The way it began,
Like the way most things begin:
A look, a single, solitary, glance.

I was happy with my illusion.
I was happy with my heavy feeling,
My solitude,
My hurt.

Then you looked at me.
When our eyes met, our souls were tied.
And the world became different.

Your glance made everything quiet.

WIND + RIVER

In this imaginary place,
There is an endless summer Where we
are together
At the edge of the river,
Your face is covered by a veil
And will, in time, be revealed.

I cannot turn my feelings away.
The wind blows by the river,
I see your smile under the veil.
The wind carries every word I want to say
The river flows with everything that I know.

I don't have anything to hide.
The wind and the river, they know everything,
They are whispering it to you beneath the veil.

I step into the river,
And raise my arms high above my head.
I dare you wind, I shout.
I dare you. Lay claim to me.

The wind does not take me, Instead it
raises your veil.

And I cannot turn away. Forever,
Expressed in every word I will ever speak
Every thought I will ever think
Brighter than any sun,
More beautiful than any flower
More than the earth, the water or the wind
More than I ever dreamed.

You step into the water
And take my hand.
The veil is gone, but the wind still blows.
Where the river will take us,
Will, in time, be revealed.

ENDLESS

Like an endless film,
Where the characters always dance, always play.
Breathing life, creating sentiment.
This is where we belong.

There is no winter here,
Only patterns formed from liquid and sunlight.
Its warm here,
This is where we belong.

If there is a God and if He takes pity on us,
Maybe he will allow us to remain
In this warm place.

In this endless film, where there is no beginning. Certainly no end
(its endless, you see)
There is only sentiment,
Sentiment expressed from life.

Here we can play forever,
Here we can dance forever.

THE BARISTA

In some forgotten coffee house,
In some forgotten corner of Venice,
I met a lonely barista.

He had sad eyes
And a rose in his lapel
His skin was turning brown,
Like the coffee served.

He told me about love and loss
Love is the greatest gift,
Take it whenever it comes.
Because if you refuse it, you never know,
One day it may refuse you too.

He talks of his angel, her name long forgotten——
but not her face and not her soul.
You will know an angel, when you see one
The Barista musters a smile at me.
They lift your soul and clean your eyes, he says.

The barista is alone now.
Alone with my coffee, he says.
In every thought, in every single moment,
I know she is with me.
He smiles, a lonely smile.
Somewhere, she is here.
She can see me,
She can feel me.

I know, he says,
I know because I feel her too.

You can always feel an angel.

HOW TO SAY IT

I want to tell you that I love you.
But I am not sure how I can express it.

I want to take you to my imaginary place
And lead you by the hand
To the pink oceans,
To the purple roses and the neon orchids.

I want to tell you.
But I am not sure if can.

Maybe I will make a film.
Maybe I will sing a song. Perhaps an
erotic dance,
Or graffiti on your heart,
Either way, I am not sure how to tell you
I love you.

What I'm trying to say is,
I know how to love you,
I just don't know how to tell you.

Would a smile be okay?
I know how to do that,
You taught me.
Remember, that time by the river,
You taught me.

I want to tell you that I love you.
So I will.

I love you.

YOUR RESONATING LIGHT

Standing up here I can see the millions of lights
Climbing like monuments in the sky.
I will stand and watch them,
Until the sun rises.

There is one more light,
A hidden light that will betray its darkness,
A light that will bring you on its back
A light that would make me wait forever.

3 AM

3 AM
Can't sleep
You're far away
Far too far away

Its cold, the leaves are falling
That affects a man's soul, you know.
Breathing the cold in my lungs
All this may lead to chaos (but hey, I wear it well)

This bitter autumn gives me the time
To think about what I want to say
At 3 AM
After the night, before the day
I know, that with you
I can stand in hope,
Like an island
Maybe one day I will be discovered,
Maybe one day I will be saved.

I, OCEAN

Like the ocean,
I want to cover you.
I want to wrap myself over every inch of you,
Every inch of that wonderful body.

I want to surround you.
I want to tease you
I want to take you
I want to be in you,
I want to be on you,
I want to be under you.

Like the ocean,
I want to carry you far away,
To exotic places,
Secret places, only we can discover.

Like the ocean,
I will protect you,
I will provide life.

Like the ocean,
You make me vast
You make me powerful.

Like the ocean,
I am yours.

JUST LIKE LEONARD

I've always wanted to be a poet,
Just like Leonard Cohen.
But I don't know where to start.
I don't know what its like
To have the life of a poet.

I've never lived in an exotic place,
All my heartbreak has been trivial (still it was rough for me)
I've never smoked cigarettes (maybe once when I was a teenager)

What is being a poet?
Is it writing poetry?
Or is it more?
Maybe it's a lifestyle.

Can I write poetry without being a poet?
Can I be a poet without writing poetry?

I can try both
I can try either
I can try neither

I've always wanted to be a poet
Or I've always wanted to write poetry
I am not sure any more
I don't know where to start

Maybe I should start with you.

FREE HUGS

Downtown,
I saw a man.
He was offering free hugs and a smile.

Nobody got near him.
They were afraid, I guess.
So, I hugged him.
And then they arrested him,
Disturbing the peace and loitering, they said.

As they took the man away, he was laughing.
All I want to do is make the world a better place, he said.
The world doesn't want to be better.
Maybe it's afraid.

WAITING

I sit
On a solitary chair
In a solitary room
There is fire on the walls
And ice on the floor.

I sit.
I wait.

The woman with the torn gown enters and smiles.
Have you been waiting for me?
No.
You should have. I can bring you pleasure.
No.

I sit.
I wait.

The little girl with the giant lollipop enters and giggles.
Does it hurt?
What?
Waiting.
No… uh, yes… well it depends on how you look at it.
That's a funny answer.
There are a lot of funny things in the world, I tell her.
I don't understand, she says.
I smile. Unfortunately, some people never will.

The old woman with the cigarette breath enters and approaches.
What are you waiting for?
I know, but I don't know.
Like a puzzle of the heart?
Yes.
Would you wait forever?
Yes.
Even if it never came? Yes.

I sit.
I wait.

THAT PERFECT NOVEMBER

That perfect November,
We were together.
Shining like diamonds in the sky
Strong like the sun.

That perfect November,
Was like heaven, with central heating.
There were no secrets,
There was nothing to hide.

That perfect November,
You were a queen
And I... I was a king.
We carried our prince to our castle in the clouds.

That perfect November
It felt like spring,
A perfect dawn for a perfect summer,
No sign of that old bastard, winter.

That perfect November
We danced on the fallen leaves
Hoping to give them life,
Racing against the fate of time.

That Perfect November
Will remain forever,
The unmoving pillar of my soul
Unchanging and immortal.

THE CITY

The city is,
A collection of broken hearts,
A collage of sad faces,
Sad, thinking, faces everywhere.

Maybe they heard about the puppy in the box
Or the little girl in the closet,
Maybe its because there is no more dawn
And the birds have stopped singing
They can see it.
Salvation buried inside retribution
The cold, black cloud full of chaos,
It's coming down, unto the city, to take all it can.
The depression, that everybody knows is there,
But, still, no one can quite explain it.

How many cry at home, praying to be saved,
Saved from the broken dreams of the city,
Saved from this nightmare, they call home?
How many of them know disorder and shame?
How many of them wish they could start again?
Ah, to start again somewhere safe and warm.

Somewhere far away from the sad, thinking faces.
Somewhere far away from the broken hearts, Somewhere far
away from the broken city.

THE LITTLE ROOM

I have this little room, where I keep all my secret things.
There is a little window, in this little room.
When the sun shines through that little window,
This room is filled with all the colors of the day.

With it, the sun brings light
Light to the shadows and dust,
The secrets are allowed to dance free in the light.
For a brief moment love, with all its secrets, will be revealed
And with dignity and grace,
It will disappear again.

MY FAILED SOUL

I've lied to you and to the world.
Swallowing the lies, like they had medicinal value.

Now, I sit on this broken chair, in the crooked corner
There are no words, there are no feelings,
There are no more places to hide. Judgment
rides in on horseback,
He's coming for me.
His fangs are ready for my soul,
To never make me forget, these things I've done.
The pain I've caused, the spirits I made dirty.

Who Am I kidding?
His presence has been looming for years.
But I guess, even if you know, it still comes as a surprise

I am at his mercy,
For all the hearts I've brought to a burning hell.
My soul is there to be scattered
Scattered over the dirty city,
With its burning destruction,
My soul is there.

If he can take my bruised and failed soul,
And if he can mold it
Into something that will make you smile
Even if only for a brief moment,
Then I will have purpose.

THE PROMISE

He made a promise
A deep and sacred promise
To stop seeing the world in black,
To shift to another color,
Maybe yellow or something like orange.

You are a traitor, they said,
After he had made the promise.
You are abandoning your own will
Foolishly hoping for redemption
No one will forgive a traitor and a fool.

Nonetheless, he carried on with his promise. Alone he went, up the tower.
What better place to see the world, he thought
He went to observe the colors of the rain.
Hoping they would wash over him,
And wash through him.
He shouted at the sky and the colored rain,
Make of me what you will.

The rain thundered over his body,
And bound his soul with its wet fist.
You are no fool, it said.
And certainly, you are no traitor.

He began to laugh.
A laughter that made him drunk,
As the rain dried
Music began to play,
And the tower felt pure. His soul
was full——
Full of color
And black, was nowhere to be found.

JOURNEY TO YOUR SOUL

I climbed the highest mountain,
I was looking for answers.
Instead, what I found there
Was a jar of vinegar.

I swam to the bottom of the deepest sea,
I was looking for the face of God.
Instead, what I found there
Was a broken tree.

I walked the greatest dessert,
I was looking for salvation
Instead, what I found there was an empty bottle.

I dove into your soul,
I wasn't quite sure what I was looking for
What I found there was everything I will ever need.

JUDGEMENT

When you're old and gone
What will your legacy be?
What will your meager existence mean?
On the grand scale of things,
What will it really mean?

You're whole life you dressed up,
Like a Halloween vampire,
Walking with your cape and fangs.
But when it's all said and done,
We're all the same, aren't we?

When its time for your number to be counted,
Will you beg for forgiveness?
Or will you stand with your choir,
And sing to the empty crowd?
Sing your song full of hollow words.

When God looks at you,
Will you stand in fear?
Or will you dance on your tippy-toes
With your red scarf and torn dress?
Dance your dance in the garden of lost souls.

When it comes time for all us to be judged,
By a power greater than we can ever know,
What will it all mean?
Will it all be revealed?
Or is existence truly so selfish?
Maybe love is the salvation of the soul,
Maybe it brings a higher existence,
A deeper understanding,
A life outside our own.

Maybe…
I guess, we'll have to wait and see.

3 AM II (OR 3 AM IN TORONTO)

3 AM,
Halloween night,
Its cold out,
But it's okay,
Tonight, I like Toronto.

Somewhere in Kensington,
A broken mariachi band plays,
For a crowd of broken drunks
Since you left,
My heart plays like their guitars,
Hollow and out of tune.

I walk the streets,
I get lost trying to find you.
The Mariachi's are still playing
While I try to fall asleep.
The out of key song brings dreams of you.

Since you left,
I have nothing left. Except
sorrow
And this hollow heart, Nothing
more.

If healing myself means forgetting you,
Then I want to stay sick.
If being lost holds onto a tiny fragment of you,
Then I'd get lost in these streets forever.

I WILL, I WOULD

You're allowed to lie to me,
I would accept it.
I would believe you,
No matter what you told me.

I will be your armor,
I will be your mask.

I would touch light for you,
Wrap it up with a pink bow
And offer it as a sacrifice to your body.

You're allowed to hurt me,
I would let you.
I would surrender.

I will be your torch,
I will be your warmth.

For all the heartbreak and the sorrow,
For anything and for everything,
Do what you will to me,
I am yours.

THE CLIFF

It feels like another lifetime now.
I was sitting at the top of the cliff.
Looking out into the distance as far as I could see.

I don't remember what brought me there.
I don't remember how long I stayed there, Watching the
shadows, and the light.

The black thoughts that poisoned my mind,
The storms of my greatest burden,
Had all passed,
Had moved away, with the clouds.

I relinquished everything,
To an understanding:
Memories are what we hold on to. Memories are
what hold on to us,
They promise, they conspire,
To make the future,
To make the past, Both
equal.

With the warm wind,
I began to forget,
My mind began to stray and wander.
Everything I had known,
Everything I had seen,
The words I had once spoken,
The dreams I once had,
Began again.

HERE

Hide it all,
Keep everything safe,
In this place,
You built.

You can stay here forever,
Its warm here,
Its safe here,
Nothing can come in.

You can be here in peace,
You can hold on to all of it.

There will never be a storm here,
There is only sunshine here.

Here you can be yourself,
Here you can be anything.

If you want it to be,
There can be nothing more real than here.

BLACK WIDOW

Her cold seduction,
Her lips say a thousand words,
Each carrying with them a thousand lies.

Her desires reveal her secrets,
Her disease.
With every single breathe,
With every single motion,
She builds the walls of hell around you.

With her mechanical disguise,
She will tear away at your soul, Claiming that
you will be free.

As she gets closer,
She will whisper,
She feels what you feel.

Sensing your broken heart,
She takes hold,
And your soul expires into the shadows.

WAKAMATSU BREAKFAST

In this land of orange moths and mountains,
Where there is nothing left,
Except the stable order of routine,
I sit on a rock
Watching the plastic women,
Wearing their mandatory smiles as they judge me.
They all know,
That I am too small to be famous
They all know,
That I am too big to sit in their chairs.

In this land of plain talking
And flashing lights,
Where one war was lost and another will begin
Here where my culture of doubt burns across a culture of
polite lies.
Here amongst everything real or not,
For better or for worse,
Ancient history meets science fiction.
The contradiction brings a certain kind of beauty to this land.

Here,
In this land where I am illiterate,
In this land that I am meant not to understand,
Here,
In this land,
I can find peace in being alone.

THE EMPTY PLACE

In this empty place,
Where time stands still
Hangs an empty picture frame,
With empty memories
Of the changing seasons.

Time stands still,
Without that old, quiet, noise
That builds the boldness of life.
This place will always be empty.

This empty place
Made me run and hide.
I wanted to change my face,
With a new face I could start again
Somewhere new and full of life,
But it didn't last.
I didn't last.

That empty place
It called to me
Like a forgotten lover,
I ran to the warm embrace of its breast,
To be alone with my empty memories of you,
To be alone with my empty happiness.

<u>L</u>

Elle m'a regardé, sans rien dire,
Et Pour un seul moment, le ciel est ouvert pour moi.

THE MONK HONDA, MY FRIEND

I sat at the temple with the monk Honda,
I want to tell you a story, he said.
I want to tell you about the fate of this place we live in.
I want to tell you about the hopelessness of it all.

He looked at me with his bright eyes
The wind will carry change to this place, he said.
On its back, the wind will bring meaning beyond anything we recognize.
Love will be more than a sad song.
What's broken will be fixed
And what's fixed will be redefined.

I want you to know, he said,
That it's not about God or even belief,
It's about each other and each of us.
If only we can face one another,
With nothing in our minds
And nothing on our lips,
How would things be then?

His eyes shone with the fury of hope.
It's not complex, he said.
In fact it's very simple,
The world is living in a closet.
Those who know, Know:

Maybe somewhere there still is light,
Maybe somewhere a voice still sings.
Maybe somewhere love is still more than a sad song.

QUEEN LOVE WITH WINGS

Where love is law
You would be queen.
All would obey your will
And I would be your shadow.

From my knees
I would abide by your every whim.
I would watch you fly.
In awe of your soul,
I've never felt anything so pure before.
You'll have to excuse me,
But near you I can only be still.

WOULD YOU

Would you believe me
If I told you that the world was ending?
Would you hold my hand until the end of time?
Would you whisper to me when no one is to make a sound?
Would you lie to me, and tell me that the world is bright with hope?
Would you look for me in the dark corner at the end of the dark cave?
Would you go to midnight mass and pray to a laughing God?
Would you beg Him to save my soul from the darkness?
Would you build a wall to hide me from the devil when he comes?
When the end comes and everything is said and done.
Would you still know who I am?

LAS VEGAS V.S. TOKYO

Las Vegas has many lights
Tokyo has more

Tokyo wins

Las Vegas is fast
Tokyo is faster

Tokyo wins

Tokyo is plastic
Las Vegas admits its plastic

Las Vegas wins

Tokyo is full of money
Las Vegas is full of real money

Las Vegas wins

Las Vegas is full of Americans
Tokyo is full of Japanese

I guess that one's a tie

THE KING AND THE PRINCE

Tickle, tickle goes the King
Giggle, giggle goes the Prince

The King smiles
And the Prince smiles

The King's the world stops.
He knows...
The honest, immovable truth:
Without the Prince,
He cannot be king.

WHERE I AM

Isn't funny how the things that make most sense,
Always seem the most difficult to achieve.

This Place,
Like a mistress with Vaseline on her lips,
Beckons me to stay.
She promises me a slow life in a fast place
She promises me assimilation through curiosity,
Instead of the familiar ignorance through self-importance.

This place,
Where I am welcomed,
Instead of being a quiet inconvenience.

This place,
That deserves much better than me,
Seems to make no sense.

This place,
That I will never understand, Seduces me
with her promises.

This place,
Is home.

REBUILT

I tried to touch heaven,
But I got cut into so many little pieces.
With your breath and warm touch,
You took the fragments and built a man.

At dawn, as the sun made the sky orange,
With the final touch of your fingers,
I was whole again.

I cannot break anymore,
You are here.
Heaven is here too.
I do not need to touch it,
It touched me.

THE LADY WITH NICE EYES

The lady with nice eyes, Drove
me in her car.
We did not speak the same language,
But somehow we understood each other.

Having never really known me,
She treated me like an old friend.
Wanting nothing more than to know me.

The lady with nice eyes, Cried
when I left.

The lady with the nice eyes, Gives me
faith in humanity.

MY TRUTH

I fall to my knees before you.
I know, the truth.
The only truth is:

You are my strength,
All of my strength.
You are my voice,
Every vowel, every verse.
You are my peace,
All of my peace.
You are my soul,
Every sin, every purity. You are
my reality,
My entire reality.
You are my happiness,
Every moment, every smile.

You are my truth, My
only truth,
You are my love,
My only love.

DOLLS

Dolls, Everywhere,
Pretty dolls.

Some made to look older,
Some made to look younger.
Yet all the same:
Plastic,
And hollow on the inside.

Dolls,
All of them,
Pretty plastic dolls,
Some of them want to be collected.
Some of them want to be owned.
All of them want to be looked at.

Dolls,
All the pretty little dolls,
Plastic and Hollow.

Dolls,
With no meaning.

Dolls,
With no soul.

HATE

I don't hate this,
I hate myself doing this.

I don't hate you,
I hate myself wanting you.

I don't hate this world,
I hate myself in this world.

MY PRAYER

Whoever is up there in Heaven,
Can you hear me scream?
Can you hear me beg?

The demon has visited this place.
He fetched her soul.
He put it in his velvet sack
And rode away with it in his black chariot.

O Heaven, hear me please!
If you can, I implore you, Bring her
soul back.
With all your power and might,
Defeat the demon and return her soul.

I am a liar and a cheat,
But I am humble.
Please understand,
Her soul is all that I have,
All that I am.

BELIEF

I want to believe in love again,
I want to believe it can save the world,
Or at least change it.

I want to believe that there can be hope again,
Hope for the future,
Hope for my son.

Anyone who knows love, True
Love,
Knows:

Anyone who knows hope, True
hope,
With nothing else to believe in,
Knows:

Hope and love are the quiet breath of the world.

SAVIOR

This war with no name,
Procrastinates and bides its time.
We the people,
Close our eyes to it all.

No path for the destruction,
No end to the chaos.
Nothing to be seen through the smoke and dust,
Nothing except you;
The one savior,
You are here now.

In this maelstrom,
All that will remain is us.
From the ashes,
We will build paradise,
We will build the future.

WINTER

The sun sets as the winter music begins to play.
The cold breeze takes the final October leaf.
The clouds fill past the moon.

Tomorrow the city will be dressed in white.
With it, maybe, the snow will bring innocence and purity,
Or at least reflect whatever light remains,
Maybe it will bring change.

THE MONK HONDA, MY FRIEND II

The monk sits on the tatami sipping his tea slowly.

He says:

People are comfortable living a lie,
It's easier to be right when you lie.
It's one of many things that are dimming the light of humanity.

The monk looks at me, he knows.

He says:

People listen to the loudest voice,
That doesn't mean the loudest voice is best.
The loudest voice simply wants to conquer.

A slight breeze washes through the room and the monk smiles.

He says:

People always want to worry
About things that waste time
All their solutions are transparent.

The monk looks at me his eyes shine like jewels.

He says:

People live their lives,
Pretending that tomorrow will never come.
The only truth people know is chaos.

The monk pours himself another cup of tea.

THE ONLY PROMISE

In my darkest nightmare,
I ran to the darkest corner,
Of the darkest cave,
And I cried.

I knew that I had failed you.
Despite all of my hopes and ambitions,
I had failed you.

If I could change the past,
I would.
If I could mold the future for you, I would.
But I cannot,
I remain powerless.

All I can promise you now,
Is uncertainty.

SOME KIND OF FORGIVENESS

It looks like you've forgiven me.
I was young I didn't know what I was doing.

You took my hand and I let go.
You believed in me
And I laughed.
I guess we're all nihilistic at that age.
Maybe I'm still a little nihilistic now,
But I'm older and I wear it better.

I had your photograph,
The only one of you I ever had,
I kept it for years, in a many number of secret places.
But in the end, it got lost.

I always knew I would find you again,
Fate is not the bitch I thought she once was,
Because I did find you and I managed to ask for your forgiveness.
You had no idea what I was talking about.
It was long ago, we were young and I was high, you said.
But hey, if it will make you feel better I forgive you.

YESTERDAY

Yesterday when the winds were cold,
Yesterday when the sun was nowhere to be seen,
Yesterday you left me standing alone on the corner,
Yesterday I lost my soul.

MY DESTINY

Alone I walked into the cave of dreams,
I looked into the lake in hopes of picking my destiny.

Was I going to be rich?
Was I going to be successful?
Was I going to be to be a genius?
Was I going to be a hero?

In the end, it didn't matter.

Looking into that lake and seeing glimpses of all that could be,
I noticed in every glimpse of every possible destiny,
You were there.

LEAF

This morning I gave my confession to a man I did not know.
I am a liar, a thief and a cheat, I said.

He looked at me with a twinkle in his eye and said:

You must live your life like a leaf floating in the wind.
Let the wind be your master,
Let it carry you where it will.
Only then will you be forgiven.
Only then will you be free.

I LOVED YOU

I loved you once.
I loved the beauty of your body.
You may not know it, buts its true.
I loved you once.

When you walked into the room, my heart raced.
When you looked at me, it felt like a dream.

Your eyes, your smile, your everything,
Was perfect.
Absolute and infinitely perfect.

So many nights I dreamt
You would wrap your perfect legs around my less that perfect body
So many nights I dreamt
Of us making love in various positions.

I tried to tell you once,
I tried to tell you I loved you.
You only smiled (maybe even laughed)
And you walked away.

I stood there and remained,
As I remain today.

THE DOCTOR

When my friend, The Doctor,
Plays the Ave Maria on his blue violin,
I remember you
And I remember how to love.

Each perfectly executed note, Brings a kiss
from your lips.

Every single articulation, Brings you
closer to me.

When my friend, The Doctor, Plays his
weeping blue violin,
I remember you
And I am healthy.

THE DRAGONFLY

I followed a dragonfly to the top of a mountain.
I looked down at the city as it sat on my shoulder,
The city is so quiet from up high.

Up on the mountain,
Life is simple and precious.

The dragonfly left my shoulder and flew down to the city.
I did not wish to follow it.
I did not want to leave my solitary requiem.

PEACE

I dare not utter words of judgment against you,
Nor I will not carry you any longer.

I simply want peace.

I will not beckon you from the shadows,
Nor will I seek out your name.

I simply want peace.

I remain powerless against your will,
But I will not scorn you.

I simply want peace.

I will no longer envelope myself in sentiments of you,
But I will never forget you.

I simply want peace.

GOD

When I was just a boy,
God came to me.
He spoke to me with warm eyes and a cold voice.
Delight in my company, He said,
It won't last long.

Come what may,
This truth will not change.
For the sins you have yet to commit,
You must walk this world alone.

What about the next world?
I asked.
God looked at me and smiled,
Then He disappeared.

GREENWASH

The planet is crying.
The planet is sick.
We're hurting her.

They drive too many cars in China,
We kill too many trees in the name of progress

These plastic bags will never decay,
They will remain as our eternal imprint on this planet.

Don't use them, we're told.
Buy something reusable,
Even if I did, it would be made in China.

The more things change, the more they stay the same.

SINCE YOU'VE BEEN AWAY

Since you've been away
The sky has been gray.

Since you've been away there's only been rain,
Yet none of it will wash away my pain.

Since you've been away I lay awake at night, Knowing
somehow that my heart isn't right.

Since you've been away the music has stopped playing,
And I sit alone talking to God and praying.

Maybe you'll come back. Maybe
you'll come back.

ALONE

When I am alone,
So alone that the world doesn't know it,
I feel at peace and free.

Nothing can harm me, Nothing
can touch me, When I am alone.

THE WINTER COLD

The winter cold is like no other heartbreak,
It is dominating and cruel.
With its apathetic hand and frozen heart,
It sweeps down and it leaves its mark on you skin and in your lungs,
It leaves its mark on your soul.

The winter cold is like nothing else,
It is the worst of all realities.
With its cruel sense of humor,
It creates a still life in a world baron and empty.

AGE

Life is funny.
First you want to escape your youth.
Later, you try to reclaim it.

Age is the only unchanging constant,
Even if you try to run from it,
In either direction, it's coming for you——
It won't let go.
It will always be there,
Like some kind of shadow to your humanity.

No matter if you wear it well or not,
It will be there.
So you might as well embrace its touch.

SLEEP FOR YOU

I know you're somewhere out there, Hidden in one
of my dreams.
Somehow, I know you're sad.
Somehow, I know you're looking for me.
Maybe if I go to sleep I can free you.
Maybe If I go to sleep we can be together.

ATTRITION

For years... so many years,
I believed I was doing things right.
And I believed I was doing the right thing.
As time moved forward,
I began losing hope
Everyday.

MY MANGLED SOUL

How I wish you were with me
Here in my mangled mind.
You could take off your black veil
And we could dance outside of the shadows.

Here, in my mangled mind,
We have nothing to fear or cry about.
Once you are here with me,
Here in my mangled mind,
The darkness will become light.

HYPOTHERMIA

My skin is like wax. My
body is numb.
I can no longer feel a thing.
My mind slows,
My thoughts drift.
Peace draws near.

The purity of this moment, Embraces
my soul.

THE GIRL WITH THE BLUE EYES

The day I first saw her,
Sitting alone in the field,
With her flower dress and the book in her hand,
I fell in love.

The sun gave her a certain glow
And the wind rustled her hair.
She looked up at me
And for an instant, time stopped.

We spoke for several hours over red wine
Maybe I was drunk, maybe not,
But we fell in love.
A wonderful and frightening feeling at the same time
It was a love that had no choice but to exist.

YOUR WORLD

In your world I am less than perfect,
I am the clown who dances to and fro
Trying to win your smile.

In your world I am a shadow,
I grace the back walls with my presence
Easily ignored by those standing in the light.

In your world I am the solitary note
Played on a long, shredded, violin,
The beauty of which is only heard by the deaf or the dead.

In you're your world I have been forgotten.

REFLECTION

Last time I looked in the mirror, There was
nothing there.
My soul has disappeared,
Leaving only a shell looking back at me.

Can you tell the difference between my reflection and me?
Which of us is it that you love?

THIS IS FOR YOU

What is it that is hiding behind your eyes?
You once told me that you live your life like the rain:
Alone and everywhere all at the same time.

Where ever it is that you fall,
I would fall with you.

My memories of you are in slow motion
And they are forever.

If you were to die,
I would follow you.

Allow me to appease you in some way.
Take my hand let me guide you.

I would cry to save you.
I would die to save you.

MY LIVELY HEART

My lively heart,
Churns like a caffeinated infection
With forgotten dreams and empty prayers.

Alone I must face every failure.
Alone I must answer for every sin.
Alone my lively heart must beat.

My lively heart,
Waits here with me,
In this shadow… Waiting
for you.

Alone I will survive. Alone I
will atone.
Alone my lively heart must beat.

TONIGHT

Tonight I lived my life like you were still there for me.
With a penny in my pocket
And 10 000 days of rain ahead of me,
I walked all night…
I walked to the end of the world,
But not to the end of my sorrow.

Tonight I walked with the right amount of danger in my heart.
I walked like the light in my eyes wasn't fading.
For brief a moment I forgot about all the unwanted memories.

Tonight I lived my life believing I still loved you.

BLIND HOPE

We divert eyes to tomorrow,
And waste our lives like our children have no future.

We pray to God that His hand will make things right,
Forgetting that He helps those who help themselves.

The world is crying
Because justice is a voice that cannot be heard
And chaos packaged nicely is still not order.

And our prayers may not be answered.
We may not be saved.
There will be no vindication.
We must suffer with our suffering

With all hope and faith,
The truth is
Judgment day may never come.

TORONTO

The streets are empty
The heroes have all disappeared
Nothing left
But a defenseless city
Cold and Afraid of its own shadow

SUBTITLED

チャンスはありますか？
Do I have a chance?
チャンスをくれますか？
Would you give me one?
ただ、あなたの魂に触れるだけ
Just one chance to touch your soul,
ただそれだけが全てです
That's all I need.

もし許されるのなら
Would you let me?
一瞬だけ
For just one moment,
あなたの手をつないでもいいですか
Would you let me hold you hand?
そうしたら
Let me take it.
あなたをどこかへ導いてあげる
And lead you away from here,
あなたを自由へと
Lead you to freedom.

知っていますか？
Do you know?
受け入れてくれますか？
Would you accept?
私自身、そして私の全てを
Me, and all that I am,
どうしようもない位不完全だけど、あなたに夢中です
Hopelessly imperfect and addicted to you.

わかってくれますか？
Do you understand?
信じてくれますか？
Would you believe?
あなたなしでは生きられない
I cannot live without you.

Why did you love me? I've been trying to figure that out, but I really don't know. I stayed awake last night remembering what we had and remembering how I hurt you. I cried as remembered our last day and our last kiss.

I did so many things wrong, but you loved me anyway.

Of course, you weren't stupid—you did leave me.

I hate you.

I am writing to tell you that I am leaving; I've decided to move to the other side of the world. I guess we both saw this coming.

The last time I saw you, you were wearing your heart on your sleeve and you cried, right there in front of everyone, you cried. I was at a loss for words, so I did the only thing I knew how to do, I ran. I turned my back on you and I ran. I've been sorry for that ever since. I guess that's why I am writing. Maybe I am looking for forgiveness, or maybe I am looking for closure.

I still have that letter you gave me, with the chocolates. Keeping these things makes me feel young again; they bring me back to that warm place where life seemed to have more faith. I guess that's why I am writing, to thank you for that simple kindness you showed me. To tell you that you affected me, you touched my soul, in a way that I am only now starting to understand.

When it all hit the fan and life put the squeeze on us, you were always the strong one; you were always there for me. You were proud of me. I guess that's why I am writing, to tell you that you are indefinably and intimately beautiful, I should of have told you when I had the chance, but I guess this will have to do.

In the secret places of my heart, I will always love you—really love you, like in those old black and white movies, the ones that didn't always have happy endings. I guess what I am trying to say that is despite my leaving, if God is kind and fate generous, we will see each other again.

Sincerely,

M.J. Di Rocco

M.J. DI ROCCO

Let me tell you about M.J.,
He's a liar and loser.
I can't stand him!
He thinks the little words he writes make some sort to sense,
He thinks he knows life and he burdens his views on everyone.
M.J. Di Rocco is a fool.

People love his stories,
M.J. confuses this for some sort of influence,
When, in truth, he is no more than some beer time anecdotes.
He thinks women love him and men want to be him,
In truth they all laugh at him behinds his back,
M.J. Di Rocco is joke.

M.J. smokes too many cigars,
He drinks too much bourbon,
He doesn't listen and he laughs funny.
M.J. Di Rocco is a child.

M.J. should give up,
He should finally accept his laziness.
He's nothing more than a lousy writer and ugly human being.
M.J. Di Rocco won't change the world.

YOU

You are there,
I am here.
That's the way it is for now.
Complications separate us.

In my mind sits a perfect memory of you,
An unchanging vision of your beauty,
A beauty that heals me,
A beauty that forgives me.

You are there,
I am here.
I want to change that.
No more complications.

I want you all to myself,
I want to take you away from here.
Where I can drink your beauty,
Until I a forgiven,
Until I am healed.

ROUTINE

I am tired
And everything looks the same,
Every face,
Every street.

I forgot where I am.
My heart longs for change,
Yet it also longs for home.

I am tired
And everything feels the same,
Every forced laugh,
Every fake tear.

I forgot what life feels like.
I no longer want to be empty.

I cried when I thought that I would have a chance to love you.
In that one thought,
In that one brief moment,
I felt immortal and free.

I am trying to bury this life
And start a new one—a new life far away.
But I can't,
The memory of you won't let me,
It's trapped me here in the walls of your blacked soul.

AYLMER

I lived in Montreal too long,
It made me sarcastic and hard.

I lived in Toronto too long,
It made me stoic and apathetic.

I lived in Aylmer for only a year,
I found my soul.

41

I look at the bus driver,
I wonder if he always wanted to drive the number 41?

I look at the lady pouring my coffee,
She's in her 50s, pouring it black into the paper cup.

I looked at the man pushing his shopping cart,
He moves slowly along the boulevard.
His shoes have holes and he smells of beer.

The world is 95% broken dreams.

Why is just getting by enough?
Why is doing your best not enough?
Things needs to change.

WORDS FROM A WITHERED SOUL

- Maybe it's best if our children never discover the burden they carry—the burden set out by their ancestors.

- Because we are flawed, life will, inevitably, never be perfect. Life's beauty, however, lies in its constant, subtle changes and evolution.

- A man talks to God and prays for forgiveness and joy despite having done nothing of any significant in his life.

- Stop trying to change the world. Stop trying to make a difference. Be the best person you can be—if we all do that the world will indeed change and the difference will be felt.

STAY

Don't go,
Please.
I need you here next to me,
You're all I've got.

Okay, if you need to go,
I understand.
But can you leave, at least, a shadow of your soul?
A shadow I can love.

I cannot go where you are,
I want to, but I cannot.
The distance and time between us;
They define us,
They carry our souls,
They are all we will ever be:
Beautifully imperfect
And compassionately sad.

BELIEVE IN LOVE

I want to believe in love again,
I want to believe it can save the world,
Or at least change it.

I want to believe that there can be hope again,
Hope for the future,
Hope for my son.

Anyone who knows love,
True Love,
Knows:

Anyone who knows hope,
True hope,
With nothing else to believe in,
Knows:

Hope and love are the quiet breath of the world.

CONFUSED

You hurt me, but that's okay.
We have a lot going on and I am here for you.
I want to be, always I will be.

And it's complicated and it's painful sometimes,
But you know what?
I don't mind.
I love you. I'm addicted to you.

I'd rather cry for you than die without you.

Let me kneel here, in front of you.
Let me fill my hollow soul with your beautiful confusion.

I love you.

SHE FROM TROSS

She's hard to define,
But she defines me.

She tries to push me away,
But she's my home.

She brings me epic heartache,
But she always makes me better than before.

She let me touch her perfect body,
But her mind pours confusion upon me.

She loves me,
But she's afraid.

She might be like that forever,
But that's okay I love her.

She is my passion.
She is my throne.

LEARNING

Before I met you,
I thought I had figured everything out.
Then I heard you laugh
I looked into your eyes

And in one enormously tiny instant,
I had been redefined.

With you:

I'm learning how to love.
I'm learning that happiness isn't simple.
I'm learning that it's okay to be frightened.
I'm learning that life is beautifully complicated.
I'm learning to be stronger.
I'm learning that the answers may never come.
I'm learning that I will always be here, even if I fail or get hurt.

I'll always come back to you.
I know this is where I must be.

www.ingramcontent.com/pod-product-compliance
Lightning Source LLC
Chambersburg PA
CBHW051708040426
42446CB00008B/778